# Flying with The Birds

## Rev. Joe Williams

*The Last Original Member of the Iconic Dixie Hummingbirds*

### Dr. Lynn Peterson

*Rev. Joe Williams attending an event*

# Dedication

It is both an honor and a joy to pen this memoir of Reverend Joseph Williams.

Our journey began on September 9, 1995, when Rev. Joe officiated my wedding. I remember asking him to remove the word *"obey"* from the vows—and he did. We've laughed about that ever since.

Years later, in 2017, I heard his voice on the radio and instantly knew it was him. I turned to my husband, Wayne, and said, *"I don't think we paid him enough for our wedding."* So, we found Rev. Joe and presented him with what we believed was the "balance due."

This book is our 30th anniversary gift to Rev. Joe and Laverne Williams—a small tribute to their life devoted to God, to people, and to the preservation of true Gospel music.

May these pages serve as a glimpse into your journey, your faith, and your love. Thank you both for allowing me to share your story with me, and now with the world.

# Acknowledgments

Thank you to the friends and family of Mount Airy United Fellowship. Your love and input helped to create this keepsake and accounting of the life and times of our Pastor, Reverend Joe, and his beautiful wife, Laverne, and daughter Cydney. A Special shout-out to Tyrone Reed, Keith Howell, John Roberts, Gene Chapman, Sarge, Elder Goodman, Miss Carmen, Miss Bracy, Jackie Smith, Rhonda Scott, and so many more. This commemorative book would not have come together without you all.

Love and respect,
*Dr. Lynn Peterson*

# About the Author

A nationally certified post-secondary educator, Lynn Peterson has trained over 3,000 health professionals and holds advanced degrees in education and health sciences. She is the owner and CEO of BookWormz, LLC an eCommerce company.

As a passionate Health and Nutrition Advocate, she focuses on the health disparities impacting Black and Brown communities. Her work shows the connection between food, sickness, and health through science-backed research. She is an Educator, Researcher, Speaker, Blogger, and Podcaster. Lynn is the creator of HealthNewsViews.info & *Food the Final Frontier*, a podcast exploring chronic health issues plaguing the Community, with 4,000+ downloads. Her mission is clear: shift the conversation from awareness to action by teaching through documentation and not just conversation. The hallmark of her advocacy is an Ayurvedic proverb:

*"When the Diet is Wrong, Medicine is of No Use*
*When the Diet is Correct, Medicine is of No Need"*

# Table of Contents

Chapter 1—The Root of the Fruit..................................... 1

Chapter 2—Life's Influencers ........................................ 8

Chapter 3—The Coal Miner's Daughter ....................... 16

Chapter 4—Flying with the Birds ................................. 26

Chapter 5—Pride & Prejudice ...................................... 32

Chapter 6—The Calling ................................................ 40

Chapter 7—The Push to the Pulpit................................ 47

Honors & Accolades .................................................... 62

Rev. Joe Quotes .......................................................... 67

"For we are GOD's handiwork,

created in Christ Jesus to do GOOD works,

which GOD prepared in advance for us to
do

**—Eph 2:10**

# Chapter 1
## *The Root of the Fruit*

The final notes of a three-day gospel marathon echoed through the Southern night air. It was the last show in a string of four performances across small-town churches, community halls, and open-air revivals. The Dixie Hummingbirds—legends of gospel music—had poured out their souls once again. The crowd was electric. And now, the men were drained.

Five men and their founder climbed into the car, road-weary but soul-fed, ready for the 14-hour journey back to Philadelphia. The Dixie Hummingbirds had been electrifying audiences since 1928, commanding the stage with the same reverence as the Blind Boys of Alabama and the Soul Stirrers with Sam Cooke. They were more than a gospel group—they were the living pulse of a tradition born from struggle, faith, and jubilation.

Among them sat a young man from North Philadelphia— Joseph "Joey" Williams. He wasn't just along for the ride anymore. After years of promoting the group, making radio rounds, and selling records, and one of the *Sons of the Birds* he had finally been invited to sing with the very group that had once seemed untouchable. James B. Davis, the group's founder and uncompromising owner, handpicked Joe for induction into the iconic quartet.

The gig was a success. But as the road stretched ahead, it wasn't time for celebration. It was time for reflection and correction. Mr. Davis never wasted time. As the car pushed through the dark highway, the review began: pitch, tone, timing, what worked, what didn't, and what must never happen again. Joe didn't talk much that night. He listened, and he learned.

In that car, Joe understood something deep in his bones: being a Dixie Hummingbird wasn't about fame. It was about discipline, sacrifice, and sacred duty. Mr. Davis's word was gospel; his expectations were law. Joe was ready to meet the mark.

This moment was just the beginning. His connection to the Dixie Hummingbirds would stretch across four decades—from 1953 to 1993. But before the stage lights and national tours, before the applause and recognition, there was a boy in a small house in North Philly, a mother with big dreams for her son, and a childhood shaped by both melody and mayhem.

*"It isn't where you came from, it's where you're going that counts."*

—Ella Fitzgerald

## *The Early Years*

Joe Williams was born into struggle and hope, but carried by belief. His story began in a narrow North Philadelphia row house during the lean years of the Great Depression. His parents, like thousands of other Black Americans, had fled the Deep South in search of better opportunities in the North. The job market was whatever you could find. Women found domestic work, and men would do janitorial or factory work. There are stories about the demand for workers being so great that you could get fired at one factory and cross the street and begin working at another factory the same day. Joe's father would opt for a position delivering coal. He would later add plumber's helper as his second job. By the time Joe was born in 1939, Black unemployment in the city hovered near 50%. Racial discrimination, segregation, and systemic barriers defined everyday life.

Joe was the eldest son among six siblings. He remembers the bed they shared—three girls at the top, three boys at the bottom. Poverty was a constant companion, but it wasn't something he dwelt on. "Everyone around us was poor," he said. "We didn't know any different." What he did know was his mother's love—and her relentless belief that her son was destined for something greater. She told him so daily.

One day, a neighbor noticed the little boy with a spark and offered to give him music lessons. While other children played outside, Joe stayed in, learning the fundamentals of rhythm, tone, and discipline. At the time, it felt like a punishment. Playing outside with the other kids was a far better choice for the then-five-year-old. Later, it would feel like prophecy.

By five, he was singing as a child soloist with the Presbyterian "Children's Church of the Air." He was the youngest—and the only Black child—in a group that performed every Sunday in white churches across the city. "My mother never let me feel inferior," Joe said. "She made sure I knew I belonged anywhere I stood."

That confidence carried him into adolescence. When his voice changed at age 12, he stepped away from the children's choir and stepped into the streets, specifically, the underground platforms of the Philadelphia subway system. There, the acoustics were perfect, and the audience unexpected. Joe and a few friends turned echo chambers into rehearsal halls, singing doo-wop and rhythm and blues for the passersby who paused just long enough to nod in admiration.

Music, Joe realized, could open doors. It could get you girls. But more than that, it could get you out.

By 14, he had joined a boy's group, unknowingly following in the footsteps of gospel giants who had moved to North Philly from

Greenville, South Carolina, in 1942. The city's gospel scene was vibrant. A few of his friends had relatives in the industry. Eventually, some of them aged out, drifting toward jobs or the military. Two from the group joined the Marines. And Joe, captivated by the crispness of the uniform and the promise of distance, followed.

But his decision to enlist wasn't just about adventure.

Joe was running, not from the city, but from home.

Behind closed doors, Joe had witnessed too much. The arguing between his parents haunted him. His father's verbal and physical abuse of his mother pushed Joe to the brink. He feared that one day, someone wouldn't survive. It might be his mother. It might be him. He knew something had to give. And so, at 17, with parental consent, Joe joined the United States Marine Corps.

The uniform gave him freedom. But it also gave him focus.

His journey from child prodigy to gospel legend had begun not with a song, but with an escape. The Marines would teach him discipline. The Dixie Hummingbirds would teach him a legacy. And his mother's faith in him? That would teach him how to fly.

## DIXIE HUMMINGBIRDS' DEDICATION

Members of the Dixie Hummingbirds, from left, the Rev. J Williams, William Bright, Howard Carroll and Ira Tucker, stand front of their mural during the dedication of the Dixie Hummingbi Mural located at 815 North 15th St. on Sunday.

— PHOTO BY MICHAEL HA

# Chapter 2
## *Life's Influencers*

*"People are trapped in history, and history is trapped in them."*

— *James Baldwin, Notes of a Native Son*

Our identity is not shaped in isolation. It is molded by our surroundings—by the people we meet, the circumstances we face, and the history that breathes through each decision we make. Whether nurtured or neglected, influenced or inspired, who we become is deeply connected to those around us. Family, friends, rivals, and mentors—each plays a role in shaping our path. Their influence can either unlock doors or bolt them shut.

For Joseph Williams, that path took a sharp turn in 1956 when, at just 17 years old, he enlisted in the United States Marine Corps. The choice was driven by a mix of youthful ambition and admiration for the crisp, commanding presence of the uniform. Joe and his teenage friends from the vocal group "Gospel Stirrers" saw the Marines as both escape and opportunity—an honorable way to see the world beyond the narrow streets of North Philly.

# *The Marine Chapter Begins*

Boot camp at Parris Island, South Carolina, was nothing like Joe imagined. Until then, he hadn't fully grasped the meaning of military discipline. The days were grueling, and the nights even tougher. The verbal assaults were relentless, the physical demands unforgiving. One incident left an indelible mark—Joe was hospitalized for weeks after being brutally beaten for not making his bed fast enough.

But quitting never crossed his mind. Perseverance ran deep in his bones. After recovering, he completed his training at Camp Lejeune, North Carolina. Joe would later reflect that while Parris Island built the *body*, Camp Lejeune sharpened the *mind*. He emerged from the experience stronger, mentally and physically, claiming, "I could walk through any corner full of guys without fear."

Joe's transformation earned him a prestigious assignment: Lance Corporal in the Presidential Honor Guard, stationed in Hawaii. He was the **Right-Arm Black Flag Bearer**, he stood proudly before visiting dignitaries, one of only three Black servicemen in the entire Honor Guard unit. It was a position of precision, pride, and poise.

For Joe, no performance could rival standing in the Dress Blues under the Hawaiian sun—except perhaps performing on stage with the Gospel Stirrers. He even formed a musical group while in the Marines, harmonizing on base with fellow servicemen. The uniform may have drawn him in, but the discipline, music, and respect earned kept him committed.

# Reflections from Home

Growing up in Philadelphia wasn't particularly harsh, but it had its own challenges. Still, Joe speaks fondly of his childhood: never needing a house key because *Mom was always home*, and his mother would stand guard at the front door to carry out a thorough dress code inspection of his sister's outfits before they stepped outside. "Looking presentable wasn't optional—it was expected," Joe said with a smile.

His father, Joe Sr., was equally disciplined. A stickler for Sunday appearances, he made sure the entire family—six children— were dressed in their best for Sunday worship. Deacons and trustees at church took note each week as the Williams family exited their car, impeccably dressed, ready for Sunday worship.

Despite modest means, the Williams family was better off than many. Joe Sr. bought a new car every two years, his pride and joy. A coal delivery man by trade, he worked grueling shifts through Philadelphia's narrow streets. In freezing weather, he'd return home soaked, his overalls frozen to his body. One job was never enough when you have fathered six children. Joe Sr. was also an unlicensed plumber/plumber's helper. Union Licensing and registration were out of reach for the average Black man. Joe Sr was the go-to plumber among church and family members. He was capable and able to do the work, but all work had to be signed off by the white supervisor. It was hard, unforgiving labor, but necessary in an era with limited opportunities for Black men.

Joe's parents had been part of the Great Migration, leaving South Carolina in the 1930s in search of better lives. Like many African Americans of that era, they left behind systemic oppression in the South for the industrial promise of the North, only to find new forms of discrimination, poverty, and struggle waiting. Determined to make it, they stayed. They adjusted. And they raised a family determined to rise above the fray.

# *Burdened by Loss, Strengthened by Purpose*

Even amid love and order, hardship found its way in. Two of Joe's siblings—both in their twenties—lost their lives to drug overdoses. These tragedies cast a long shadow, threatening to dim Joe's light.

But he regrouped. He rebuilt. The Marine Corps may have shaped the soldier, but grief forged the man. Joe learned that survival sometimes means more than making it through training—it means choosing to rise when life knocks you down.

## Shaped by Service, Molded by Purpose

Joe's time in the Marines did more than build muscle and sharpen discipline, ignited a sense of purpose. He began to see life through a wider lens. Being stationed in Hawaii introduced him to cultures, customs, and people far removed from the rowhouses of Philadelphia. It was the first time he truly understood that his Black identity was not just defined by the struggle for survival, but also by pride, potential, and presence.

As one of the few Black servicemen in elite positions, Joe felt a weight beyond the flag he carried. He represented something larger: a visible reminder that excellence wasn't confined by color. This reality would stay with him long after the uniform came off.

It wasn't all ceremony and drill routines, though. During off-hours, Joe found joy and solace in music. The group he formed with fellow Marines not only brought comfort, it also served as a reminder that even in rigid institutions, there was room for soul.

Music grounded him. It kept alive the sense of belonging and connection to his roots, to the Gospel Stirrers, and to the neighborhood boys who once harmonized under streetlamps back home.

# The Power of Influence and Resistance

Joe's early life and military experience taught him this: influence is inevitable, but direction is a choice. Boot camp may have hardened him, but it didn't make him bitter. Seeing the world didn't make him forget home—it made him appreciate it more. Watching friends fall into traps—whether drug or alcohol addiction, despair, or violence—didn't paralyze him; it propelled him.

He understood the pain of watching someone fall. His siblings' deaths were not just personal tragedies—they were societal symptoms. The post-war years were filled with new forms of invisible wounds. Drugs flooded urban communities. Promises of prosperity were unevenly distributed. Yet through it all, Joe chose resilience over resignation.

This mindset would serve him later in life as a mentor, teacher, and, eventually, a pastor. But even before those formal titles, he carried an unspoken role—as an example. He learned to walk with dignity, even when he was the only one doing it. Especially then.

## *Legacy of the Uniform*

In later years, Joe often returned to the lessons of his Marine days—not to glorify the hardship, but to highlight the transformation. He would say, *"The uniform taught me how to carry myself, but life taught me how to carry others."*

To younger men, he emphasized that strength isn't proven by dominance but by the ability to uplift. He saw himself in many of them—young, eager, sometimes angry, unsure where to place their energy. Joe encouraged them to look beyond their zip codes, beyond peer pressure, beyond temporary highs. He taught that while we are all influenced by someone, the power lies in choosing which influence we allow to take root.

*MAMA- Dixie Hummingbirds*                    *US Marine Corps*

# Chapter 3
## *The Coal Miner's Daughter*

Christmas was always special in the Jones household. The five children could hardly contain their excitement—the familiar aromas of roasted turkey, pies, and cakes filled the home. Laughter danced through the rooms as gifts were wrapped and unwrapped with care. Mom and Dad did their best to make the holiday feel magical, even with modest means. Four daughters and one son—each knew their chores and shared in the rhythms of life.

Life in their small coal mining town was simple: school, work, and church. Two rows of houses—about twenty in all—stood in quiet formation. The Black families lived in the back row, the white families in the front. There was no debate or defiance—it was just the way things were.

Shopping meant a trip to the company store. Owned by the mining company, it sells everything: food, furniture, clothing, personal items, even cars. Paychecks were cashed there, rent was paid there, and postage stamps were purchased there. The company owned not just the store, but nearly every part of life.

# Flying with the Birds

The air was cold and crisp. Even now, the scent of burning coal still lingers in memory.

Life in the coal mining town was governed by the rhythm of the mine. Sirens rang out to signal shift changes. Black lunch pails clanked as men shuffled down the road before dawn, returning home with faces and hands darkened by soot. Every family knew what it meant to wait for their loved one to return, especially on days when cave-ins, explosions, or equipment failures made the evening news.

The Jones family, like many others, lived under the unspoken but ever-present tension of racial separation. In school, Laverne kept her head high despite being the only Black child in many of her classrooms. She recalls a story when in the 3$^{rd}$ grade the neighbor, a few years older than herself, walked to school together. One morning Laverne would get her first glance of racism. The two girls had walked to and from school for the last year. Laverne was in the 2$^{nd}$ grade and the neighbor in the 6$^{th}$ grade. That Spring Day the little girl declared, "Laverne you are Black and I am Jewish. We can no longer walk to school together", she declared.

Both girls, ignorant to the adult reasoning of the new rule, walked with distance from each other upon leaving the house, and once out of view of the block they regrouped for the rest of the walk to school. In stores, there were glances that lingered too long or service that came too slow. Black men were allowed into the mines but rarely promoted. Church was the one place where Black families could breathe freely, worship openly, and be themselves.

And still, joy persisted. Children played games, and girls learned to cook and bake. In the yards between houses, women swapped stories over laundry lines, and holiday gatherings brought out the best in every cook and choir. Despite the dangers of the mine and the racial barriers outside their door, the Jones household was full of music, laughter, structure, and love.

The Jones family had come north from Petersburg, Virginia, in search of opportunity. By the late 1930s, coal was king, and Pennsylvania needed workers. Laverne's father was among a small group of Black men employed in the mines. "I believed Daddy could do anything", she recalls. He was strong and had equal strength in both arms. She explained that in the coal mine you never knew if you had to dig on the left or the right. "Dad was an expert at arm wrestling", she said. Her brother, his friends would lose to this formidable contestant. "No, one could beat him. Every year he would take his car apart and soak the parts in gasoline to clean them. After a few days he quietly and with precision reassembled the car to the factory standards.

She recalls their first home in Leckrone and later a slightly larger house they moved into by the time she reached second grade. That house in Uniontown would be Home until she turned eighteen.

The girls made their own music—church songs in four-part harmony. Their world was a steady rotation of school, home, and church. "That's all we did," Laverne says, "was go to church." At St. Paul's AME, they often sang acapella, rehearsing for programs that filled the pews. There was one street of Black store owners and a barbershop. Near the barber shop there was a bar on the same street. But their parents forbade the children from going down there. They were warned. "Absolutely not."

Despite the segregation of the town, the Jones children attended desegregated schools. She became the third Black cheerleader in the school's history while in high school. June 1958, Laverne graduated high school, and one by one, the children began to leave the coal town in search of better lives. The mines were slowing down. Her brother, who had served in World War II, returned and was encouraged by a friend to come to Philadelphia. Her older sister earned a cosmetology license there. Laverne planned only a two-week visit but never returned home to stay.

City life opened her eyes. She'd never been to a hair salon before—her sisters always did each other's hair. She had never eaten outside her mother's cooking. She was stunned to see high school girls in makeup and jewelry. Just beyond her sister's back door stood a church—Greater Ebenezer Baptist Church. Cross the street, climb the steps, and you were inside. It was there she would meet the man she's now spent 64 years with.

Music filled the 1950s. Doo-wop, gospel, and rock and roll shaped the airwaves—Lee Andrews & The Hearts, Frankie Avalon, Chubby Checker, the Ward Singers, the Sensational Nightingales, and the Dixie Hummingbirds.

Laverne became close friends with the pastor's daughter. The pastor, Rev. L.T. Lewis, had a son who was often accompanied by a young Marine and gospel singer—Joe Williams. He always seemed to be at the church when Laverne was there. Her sisters teased her, "Who is that guy who keeps showing up every time you do?"

She shrugged. "He's friends with the pastor's son."

Joe would later admit he came to see her. But Laverne wasn't interested— "He was loud and talked too much!" she laughs now. "And he's still loud and talks too much!"

To Joe she was a lot different than the other girls. Quiet, plain dressing and always seem to be wearing gloves. Yet, in time, he captured her heart. They became engaged, and after two years, they married. It would be a June wedding. Joe was still in the Marines and needed to finish school and get a job.

Eight years into their marriage, still living in a small efficiency-style apartment, they received unexpected news: they were expecting a baby. Joe was so thrilled he ran out to buy cigars, forgetting Laverne in the exam room. She had been told she couldn't conceive. The apartment they shared did not allow children. Joe being the forward-thinking spouse decided, it was time to look for a house before the baby arrived. He spotted new homes being built just around the corner from their apartment. They never toured the home—just peeked through the windows and decided, *That one.* Joe's employer helped fudge the start date on his job so they could qualify for the home. Their first Christmas as parents was spent there—with baby Cydney, their miracle, as the gift under the tree.

They still live in that house today—57 years later.

But with triumph comes heartbreak. When Cydney turned twelve, her wish for a baby brother came true—Joey III. Born prematurely, his tiny body struggled to hold on. The family visited the hospital every day. Joe, quietly, had been visiting each morning before work.

Joey wore clothes embroidered with his initials. Nurses from other floors came to admire this beautiful baby boy. But something was wrong. Joey spent five months in the hospital. One day Laverne noticed a bruise on his thigh. His ankle was marked, too. One day, she asked why the incubator had been turned off. A nurse insisted it hadn't been turned off until Laverne held up the disconnected cord.

Then came the cast—wrapped from the baby's leg up to his diaphragm. A cast? For a non-ambulatory infant?

Joe remembers hearing Joey cry in pain from the moment the elevator doors opened. The questions piled up, but answers never came. That night, they went home shaken. Later, the call came, and Joey was gone.

Laverne and Joe retell this story as though it happened yesterday. The cast is still in the house. His tiny, monogrammed clothes are still tucked away. The ache never left. For decades, Laverne never looked at Joey's death certificate. As recent as a year ago, during a conversation with a nurse, the nurse asked: "What does the certificate say?" She admitted, "I never looked at it."

She went back and read it.

"Premature birth complications."

No mention of the broken femur. No note about the cast. No acknowledgment of the mother's request to remove it. Forty years later.

She whispers now, more to herself than anyone else: My GOD. Peace, be still.

# A Time to Mend the Fence

Joe Jr. and Joe Sr. had both grown over the years. The wounds that once drove Joe Jr. to enlist in the Marines had slowly given way to something softer—compassion and respect. The military had sharpened the young man, shaping his discipline and character. For Joe Sr., time had also reshaped him. Watching his eldest son leave home in uniform, then marry and build a life of his own, softened the man whose earlier years had been marked by hardship and silence.

The death of two of his six children brought Joe Sr. to a reckoning. Grief broke through where pride once stood rigid, and something tender grew in its place.

Unbeknownst to Joe Jr., his father had been boasting quietly to friends and neighbors about how proud he was that his son had become a Marine and was now singing with the legendary Dixie Hummingbirds. Yet, he never found the words to say it directly to his son. That silence, even today, still echoes in Joe Jr.'s memory.

In time, though, there was healing. Joe Sr. became a deacon at church, finding renewed purpose in his faith. Joe Jr., in turn, took great pride in dressing his father in fine Sunday suits, walking beside him on those sacred mornings. No words were needed. The gesture spoke volumes. Bygones were truly bygones. The Fence has been mended.

*Rev Joe and Laverne Williams Wedding Day*

*Family Photo—Wedding Day*

# Chapter 4
## *Flying with the Birds*

By the mid-1950s, the Dixie Hummingbirds had already spent 25 years building a legendary name in gospel music. However, for a wide-eyed teenager in Philadelphia named Joe, they weren't just a famous group; they were destiny. At just fourteen, Joe declared that he *had* to be part of them. He loved music, yes, but he also remembered saying with a chuckle, "That's how you got the girls if you could sing."

Drawn in by the rhythm and rise of Black music in the 1950s, Joe initially had his sights set on rock and roll or rhythm and blues. Gospel wasn't on his radar. So, when someone asked if he wanted to join a gospel group, he froze. "I don't know anything about gospel," he replied. Still, he and a few school-aged boys had been harmonizing on street corners and subway platforms, mimicking the radio hits of the day. Sometimes, commuters would pause and give an approving nod, but mostly, the boys sang for the joy of it.

Joe was eventually asked by a friend to help form a gospel group. Though he had years of musical training, his background was rooted in traditional Presbyterian church music. As a child, he sang solos with the *Children of the Air* from age five to twelve. Back then, singing came with strict rules: stand still, don't move, and if a fly landed on you, don't flinch. Gospel, with its soulful depth and free-flowing power, was another world entirely. One mentor even warned him, "Don't sing rock 'n roll and gospel—it'll ruin your voice."

One night at the Metropolitan Opera House (MET) in Philadelphia—a known hub for gospel performers—Joe overheard a man tell a young boy, "You look just like your father." Curious, Joe asked the boy, "Who is your father?" The answer stunned him: the boy was the son of James B. Davis, founder and owner of the Dixie Hummingbirds. Joe invited him to join his group. As fate would have it, another boy at the same event turned out to be the son of the group's bass player. Two direct connections to the Dixie Hummingbirds? Joe took it as a sign.

Emboldened, Joe approached Mr. Davis himself to ask if his son could sing with their new group. Mr. Davis replied honestly, "I don't even know if he can sing or not." But before granting permission, he asked a more important question: "Are the boys in your group good boys?" A quick "Yes" rolled out of Joe's mouth.

The boys became known as the Gospel Stirrers (not to be confused with Sam Cooke's earlier group of the Soul Stirrers, a similar name). As they grew older, one by one, the members enlisted in the military. This was an opportunity for each of them to go see the world. Recruiting offices were eager to get new potential soldiers, and in North Philadelphia, the selection was plentiful.

Joe had served three years with the U.S. Marine Corps. When he returned and hoped to rejoin the group, he discovered that new members had taken their place. Disappointed but not discouraged, a popular gospel disc jockey suggested they reinvent themselves with a nod to their roots: The group became *The Sons of the Birds*. Joe had written a letter to Mr. Davis requesting an opportunity to go on the road with them as *the Sons of the Birds.*

After a lot of soul-searching and scrutiny, the request was granted, and the *Sons of the Birds* began to travel as the opening act for the Dixie Hummingbirds. They recorded an album and several singles with Peacock Records in the early 1960s. Still, Joe couldn't shake the influence of the Dixie Hummingbirds. Their precision and performance style lived in his mind. That legacy would soon become his reality. Over time, Joe would be invited to travel with the Dixie Hummingbirds themselves. He spent 30 years in the presence of the elder group. Joe was the last member ever hired directly by James B. Davis and the first new hire in 37 years. Mr. Davis trusted him not just as a performer but as a representative. Joe had traveled with him to radio stations to promote concerts and was in charge of selling records at intermissions and after shows. Joe knew Mr. Davis's expectations.

# Flying with the Birds

Joining the Hummingbirds meant more than just singing. It meant living by a strict code of conduct established by Mr. Davis decades earlier. No smoking, no drinking, no swearing. No hanging out near bars or using public payphones outside questionable establishments. Their appearance had to be spotless: suits never worn offstage, street clothes neat and respectable. Even a torn seat cover in a personal car drew a stern lecture. To Mr. Davis, perception was everything. Discipline was sacred. And it paid off—the group had thrived since 1928.

"Flying with the Birds" meant weekend marathons of 3 to 4 shows in two or more towns—all packed into Friday through Sunday. Most trips were down South, often starting with a 12 to 14-hour drive from Philadelphia. Gospel Groups flourished South of Washington, D.C., while choirs ruled the North. During road trips, the group rotated drivers every two hours. Six men in a car, driving all night, singing all day. The Dixie Hummingbirds were top liners on the bill. They had sung with many of the greats in gospel and earned top billing. The Sons of the Birds were the opening act.

Joe's official induction into the original Dixie Hummingbirds came in 1983. His first event was about to take shape. The Philadelphia 76ers were playing the Los Angeles Lakers in the fourth game for the championship. The Birds were in Inglewood, NJ. They were preparing to sing at a church there the same night. A call from *Wide World of Sports* was about to change things. The caller said we would like the Dixie Hummingbirds to sing a song during the halftime break of the NBA Championship game held at the Forum in Los Angeles. This would be the fourth game of five if the Philadelphia 76ers beat the Los Angeles Lakers.

Joe got the call. They needed an answer right away because they would have to send a crew to record and splice in the recording before halftime. Joe, still new, accepted the invitation—though he didn't technically have the authority to say yes.

Right there in the basement of the Inglewood church, the Birds created, rehearsed, and recorded *"Moses is Going to Take Us to the Promised Land."* In hindsight, it was the right decision.

The inspiration for the song came by way of Sixers Center, 27-year-old Moses Malone. The performance was aired nationally on *Wide World of Sports*. That night, the Sixers defeated the Lakers 115–108 in Game Four, winning the 1983 NBA Championship. Moses Malone was named Finals MVP. Sadly, it would be the Sixers' last championship to date.

Joe later recalled the electricity of that night, the roar of the crowd, the blinding lights, and the way the song seemed to lift everyone's spirits. He felt like the music had power beyond performance. For him, that moment marked a turning point: a culmination of his youthful dream and a glimpse into the impact gospel music could have on the world stage.

The Dixie Hummingbirds sang not just with harmony but with conviction. Each stage appearance was a sermon in itself. Joe began to feel something stirring in his soul, a shift from the thrill of applause to a deeper purpose. Offstage, he found himself more drawn to community work and conversations about faith. Something was calling.

Reverend Joe would end his musical journey with the Dixie Hummingbirds in 1993, choosing to follow another divine calling—one that would take him into the next chapter of his life.

*Rev Joe's 50th Birthday Laverne, Cydney (daughter) Rev Joe Cydney & Laverne*

# Chapter 5
## *Pride & Prejudice*

In the 1950s and 60s, Philadelphia's Black population expanded rapidly due to the Great Migration. By 1960, African Americans made up about 20% of the city's population. Yet despite this demographic shift, employment remained deeply segregated. Most Black men were relegated to service, janitorial, and low-wage industrial jobs. Access to government roles and white-collar positions in banks, insurance, and municipal services was systematically denied. Labor unions, often dominated by white leadership, restricted Black membership, preventing access to skilled, better-paying trades.

By 1963, frustration with these exclusionary practices gave rise to organized protests and boycotts targeting companies like Tastykake, Sun Oil, Trailways, Coca-Cola, and Pepsi-Cola. Civil rights activists demanded change not only in the private sector but also within city departments such as police, fire, sanitation, and public offices. These protests had teeth. Under immense public pressure and legal scrutiny, businesses and city officials—including Mayor James H. J. Tate and later Mayor Richardson Dilworth—

were forced to revise hiring practices and introduce "equal opportunity" employment policies.

Among those poised to seize these long-denied opportunities was Joe Williams. With an honorable discharge from the United States Marine Corps and a natural gift for connecting with people, Joe was an ideal candidate for the new wave of jobs opening to Black men. In 1963, Pepsi-Cola hired four Black route sales drivers in the Philadelphia region—Joe was one of them. It was a moment of triumph, not just for Joe but for his family, neighbors, and the broader Black community. Strangers would see his Pepsi uniform and stop to congratulate him. His hiring represented hope actualized, a dream long deferred finally within reach.

Joe understood the weight of his presence. Being one of the first meant carrying the expectations of an entire race. "Being good wasn't good enough. Being the best was required," he once said. His performance would either affirm or negate future hires. That pressure didn't rattle him. Joe embraced it. He carried with him generations of Black folk who dreamed of a time when overcoming the odds finally came to fruition.

As a route sales driver, Joe's responsibilities were extensive: writing customer orders, maintaining delivery records, soliciting new accounts, and handling complaints. His large territory gave him room to dream—and achieve. Most customers loved him, but not all. Some longtime clients resisted the change. "What happened to Harry? Whatever you're sellin', I ain't buyin'," one store owner scoffed. Joe met resistance with resilience, continuing to make sales and quietly shifting minds.

He especially enjoyed the open road—listening to gospel or R&B on the radio and reciting scripture under his breath while winding through neighborhoods he never thought he'd be allowed to enter, let alone service professionally. One day, he made a delivery to a neighborhood grocery store only to be told, "I don't do business with coloreds." He stood there in uniform, clipboard in hand, the consummate professional, and said, "Well, today might be your first."

There was one goal that kept him motivated—a car. He had his eye on a convertible Pontiac, the kind of car that turned heads. When he asked a dealership salesman how much gas it would take to keep the car running, the man replied, "If you have to ask that, then you can't afford this car." Rather than discourage him, it lit a fire. Joe learned Pepsi was offering $25 commissions for every vending machine placed. He calculated that four machines a month meant $100—which is exactly what he needed for the car note. Joe bought the car, drove it through his neighborhood, and became a symbol of possibility. He targeted stores on Philadelphia's affluent Main Line, telling owners they could use vending profits to help with their grandchildren's college tuition. "It worked every time," he said.

Joe's confidence and drive did not go unnoticed. He frequently interacted with an administrative operator at the Pepsi bottling plant while resolving customer issues. Their professional rapport grew. But someone higher up took notice and objected. Without warning, both Joe and the white female operator were fired. There was no hearing, no appeal, and no explanation beyond the unacceptable implication of their communication. The company made no distinction between friendly cooperation and forbidden familiarity.

Joe was devastated. He hadn't even met the woman in person. He returned home ashamed, defeated, and hurt. His wife, Laverne, consoled him, but the wound ran deep. It wasn't just about a lost job—it was a betrayal of the pride he carried in wearing that uniform. He sought guidance from local pastors, hoping someone could advocate for him. None were equipped to challenge a corporate giant like Pepsi. But one name kept coming up—Cecil B. Moore.

Cecil B. Moore, president of the Philadelphia NAACP and a fellow Marine veteran, had built a reputation as a fearless civil rights warrior. Known for confronting discriminatory institutions head-on, Moore had taken on unions, city departments, and major corporations alike. Joe made his way to Moore's office. The waiting room was packed with others in search of justice. Smoke curled in the air as future lawyers and mentees buzzed around stacks of legal documents. When Joe was finally ushered in, Moore listened to his story intently. There were plenty of cases to take on, but this one seemed to have lit a fire in Moore's mind.

After a pause, Moore looked Joe squarely in the eye and said, "Are you willing to fight? Then, sit down. If you're not, get the hell out of my office."

Joe sat down.

That moment marked the start of a profound relationship. While Moore investigated the case, Joe became his personal driver. Through that position, Joe witnessed the inner workings of civic power and social activism. He saw Moore and the Reverend Leon Sullivan lead massive campaigns that held corporations and public agencies accountable. They didn't ask for change—they demanded it. Boycotts, picket lines, and media coverage followed wherever they set their sights.

Joe recalled one late-night ride with Moore after a fiery speech at City Hall. "You don't owe anyone an apology for existing," Moore said. "You walk into those boardrooms like you belong— because you do." That wisdom became a cornerstone of Joe's professional life.

Moore took up Joe's case and won. Not only was Joe reinstated at Pepsi-Cola, but he was also promoted to District Manager—in New York City.

The promotion came with new challenges. Commuting to New York was grueling, but the racial hostility was worse. One colleague remarked, "Nothing is worse than seeing a Black man in a suit—except seeing a Black man in a suit with a briefcase." Joe ignored the insults. He never allowed the ignorance of others to chip away at his confidence. From the time he sang as the only Black boy in the "Children of the Air" Presbyterian choir, Joe had learned to walk with his head high.

Corporate life brought new hurdles. In one staff meeting, the discussion turned to marketing strategy. Joe asked how Pepsi expected its salespeople to promote the brand to store owners. A manager replied, "Just use that nigger talk." He and a Latino Manager would work together in Spanish Harlem. They expected more from their managers but realized they were in a make-it-or-break-it club. It was sink or swim. They decided to swim. Breaking barriers has never been easy. Joe was the 'Jackie Robinson' of his industry.

Joe said nothing. He didn't need to. His work spoke volumes. He became one of the best-performing district managers in the region.

This chapter of Joe's life wasn't just about a job; it was about legacy, perseverance, and rising above prejudice with pride intact.

*Rev Joe accepts an Award for Howard Carroll, Sen Vincent Hughes*

# Chapter 6
## *The Calling*

*"Many are called, but few are chosen."*

— Matthew 22:14

Joe Williams was no stranger to movement. From the rhythm of gospel harmonies to the clackety-clack of trains between Philadelphia and New York, his life pulsed with sound, travel, and responsibility. He had carved out a solid life—husband, father, provider, performer. On the surface, everything looked picture-perfect. Yet something intangible hovered—a restlessness, a fog, a feeling that he was missing the very thing he was born to do.

Joe's weekdays were spent pounding pavement in New York City as a Sales Representative for Pepsi Cola. A rising star in the company, Joe managed a growing territory, drove record revenue, and was quietly observed for promotion. Each morning, he boarded the train in Philadelphia, suited up with purpose and pride, and headed north to the city that never slept. But even as he closed deals and boosted market share, something gnawed at him. It wasn't just fatigue. It was spiritual.

Weekends brought a different kind of fulfillment—singing with the Sons of the Birds. The harmonies were tight, the crowd's electric. Cities across the South—Charlotte, Columbia, Atlanta—welcomed them with open arms. Joe's voice, a rich tenor dipped in soul and truth, captivated thousands. The stage offered a rush no sales report could rival. But as the group's popularity soared, so did the demands on his time. Long drives, late nights, early mornings—life became a blur.

The toughest days were Mondays. Most started with Laverne meeting Joe at the curb outside their home just as his car pulled into Philly, fresh from a weekend tour. She'd lovingly hand him a thermos of hot coffee and usher him to the North Philly train station. A kiss, a sigh, and Joe was off again, headed for the city grind. When he returned late in the evening, she'd have a warm meal ready, and after a quick shower, he'd collapse into bed only to rise and repeat.

This cycle went on for nearly two years. Even his supervisors at Pepsi noticed. One of them, concerned for Joe's well-being, arranged for a full week's stay at the Waldorf Astoria. "You need a break, man," he told him. Another suggested finding a small apartment in the city. Joe and Laverne agreed. Maybe easing the travel would ease the tension.

On a spring Friday, Laverne took the train to Manhattan to join Joe for a tour of a potential apartment. That day would mark a turning point in Joe's life.

Before heading to pick her up from the station, Joe swung by the car wash. His turquoise-blue 1964 Pontiac convertible with the white top gleamed in the sun. That car was his pride—an emblem of hard work and perseverance. After a quick stop at the Pepsi office to check for messages, Joe heard someone yelling from below: "Joe! Joe! Your car is on fire!"

He bolted downstairs. Flames devoured the vehicle. In minutes, nothing was left but scorched metal and melted plastic. The white convertible top had vanished, and the steering wheel had liquefied. Joe stood frozen, stunned. "I had just gotten out of the car," he kept repeating to himself.

A uniformed officer stood nearby, seemingly indifferent. Joe rushed over. "Officer, someone set my car on fire! Did you see anything? Can you help?"

The officer looked at him and said flatly, "Son, in New York, we don't see anything."

The blaze felt symbolic. Like a message written in smoke. All at once, everything Charlie—the friendly shoeshine man near the Hotel Theresa—had said a few weeks earlier came flooding back.

"Maybe this is what you should be doing," Charlie had told him after hearing Joe talk passionately about singing. At the time, it felt like a casual comment. Now, it felt like prophecy.

To make matters more surreal, Pepsi was embroiled in the longest soft drink strike in New York's history. Over 200 days and counting. Bottling operations ceased. Trucks stood abandoned. Thirty-two thousand retail outlets in Manhattan, Brooklyn, Queens, and the Bronx were dry. The plant sat like a ghost town. And Joe, once full of ambition, now saw the cracks in the company's glossy exterior—discrimination, exclusion, unspoken rules about how far a Black man could go.

That Monday, Joe walked into the Vice President's office and handed in his two-week notice. He did not waver. He had seen too much and felt too much to turn back. "This isn't my calling," he said to himself. "It's time."

Back in Philadelphia, change greeted him like an old friend. No more punishing commutes. No more invisible ceilings. He wasn't just returning home; he was returning to purpose.

Philadelphia in the mid-1960s was a city in motion. Beneath the surface of its skyline and cobblestone streets pulsed a grassroots movement of progress and defiance. Civil rights leaders like Rev. Leon H. Sullivan were challenging the status quo and offering hope through opportunity. Joe Williams knew him. Everyone did. Rev.

Sullivan wasn't just a preacher; he was a visionary. A lion in the pulpit and a strategist in the boardroom.

After organizing mass boycotts of businesses with racist hiring practices, Sullivan founded the Opportunities Industrialization Center (OIC). His dream? To train Black men and women in trades and business skills that would shatter the economic glass ceilings above them. But OIC was more than job training—it was spiritual renewal.

"Teach them to believe in themselves," Rev. Sullivan would say. "Erase the lies that told them they were less." Pride and dignity were part of the curriculum.

Joe joined the movement, becoming an instructor at OIC. His years in corporate America made him a powerful figure in the classroom. He could speak fluent "business" while still walking with the people. He didn't just teach sales and marketing; he taught survival. He became a mentor, a coach, a mirror of possibility.

Unlike the rigid corporate world, here Joe could be fully himself. No suits to hide behind. No quotas to chase. He was seen. Valued. Respected. "This was what I was born to do," he would later say.

Still, Joe didn't abandon the music. He continued performing with the Sons of the Birds and often opened for the Dixie

Hummingbirds. His name rang out on Southern radio stations, and his voice brought in the crowds. Promoting record sales and booking shows became a second hustle—and a spiritual release.

Joe's calling wasn't a single moment—it was a series of divine nudges. A flaming car. A shoeshine prophet. A company strike. A city on fire with change. Some might call it a coincidence. Joe called it God.

For Joe Williams, "The Calling" wasn't just about walking away from a job. It was about walking toward purpose. Toward people. Toward a life where his gifts could multiply, not just for himself but for his community. The fog that once clouded his path had lifted. And what lay ahead was clear: A road paved not with applause or promotions, but with purpose. That purpose would be redefined. A chance meeting at a local radio station was about to change everything.

*Vocal Group Hall of Fame & Museum, Ira Tucker & Rev Joe*

*City Hall-Philadelphia recognizes Rev. Joe for Contributions to the City.*

# Chapter 7
## *The Push to the Pulpit*

The journey to the pulpit was anything but linear. Joe Williams still had one foot anchored in gospel music's traveling ministry. Weekends were filled with harmonies and hallelujahs, the rhythm of the road, and the echo of applause. But come Monday morning, his ritual resumed—dropping off records to radio stations, checking in with promoters, and greeting longtime supporters of the music he loved. It was a routine that blended showmanship with servanthood, a balance Joe had mastered over the years.

One such stop brought him to Louise Williams-Bishop, Philadelphia's First Lady of Gospel on the airwaves. A loyal friend and fierce fan of the Dixie Hummingbirds, Louise had once dubbed Joe and his group "The Sons of the Birds," honoring the next generation carrying the torch. Joe admired her voice, not just the one used on-air, but the one she used for advocacy. They spoke often about the power of music, the struggle for justice, and what it meant to be a vessel for something greater than oneself.

That day, Louise pointed through the studio glass.

"Joe," she said, "you need to meet that woman."

Standing on the other side was Mattie Humphrey—unapologetic and unforgettable. She held degrees in nursing, hospital administration, and law. None of which would quell the deep-rooted hurt, anger, and sorrow for the loss of her son. Mattie had turned the grief of her son's death in prison into a mission of reform. She was a woman who had stood toe-to-toe with city officials and never blinked. Her voice cut through red tape, her presence stirred rooms. Mattie's son, along with four others, had been severely beaten at the prison. Her son died from his injuries sustained during that incident. It was at that same prison that Mattie began her advocacy. His death ignited a wildfire in her spirit.

"Joe Williams of the Dixie Hummingbirds," she said without preamble, "what are you doing tonight?"

"Tonight?" Joe blinked. "Nothing I can think of."

"Good. You're coming to the prison. I've got two groups of men who need you. You're going to teach them everything you know."

Joe hesitated. "I don't know anything about the prison system. And to be honest, I'd rather keep it that way."

But resistance melted under Mattie's relentless purpose. She gave him a look that said, "God already said yes, so what are you waiting for?" That evening, Joe stepped into a prison classroom filled with lifers—men who had lost everything but their voices. The room was tense. Joe was cautious. He'd faced crowds, but never quite like this. But music breaks barriers.

He began with the basics—how to hold a note and how to blend in harmony. What began as technical instruction turned into something spiritual. By the end of that first session, the men surrounded him, not in confrontation, but gratitude. Joe stepped back, unsure of how to receive such raw emotion from strangers behind bars. But this moment would mark the beginning of a ten-year ministry.

What began as harmony became healing.

Men who once scowled in silence now sang through tears. Joe didn't just bring music, he brought ministry. He listened. He prayed. He sang with them, not to them. Attendance grew from a handful to hundreds. Over time, Rev. Joe never asked why a man was incarcerated. That wasn't his mission. His assignment came from Matthew 25: "I was in prison, and you visited me."

It was within those walls that Joe's true calling became undeniable.

He began taking theology courses at night and during downtime between gigs. It wasn't about earning a title. It was about understanding the Word more deeply. Laverne, always his sounding board, encouraged his studies and reminded him of the responsibility that came with the pulpit.

Ordination followed. But not without questioning. Joe wrestled with the idea of leaving the stage, of trading in the spotlight for sermon notes. Joe was confronted by the leadership of the Dixie Hummingbirds. You must decide, "Sing or Preach". The joy he found walking through the prison gates—each time greeted by voices ready to worship—reassured him he was on the right path. Joe officially left the group he had loved and admired for 50 years. The stage, the lights, the applause, and road trips were now going to be little more than a passing memory. Joe had a higher calling. Flat-footed and focused, the change would begin.

One evening, Laverne asked a life-altering but straightforward question:

"What happens when they're released, Joe? Where do they go? Who welcomes them home?"

That question lingered like incense. Joe couldn't shake it.

Out of that conversation came the vision for Mount Airy United Fellowship. Not just a church, but a refuge. A place where coats and shoes were given freely. Where meals were served without judgment or red tape. Where sermons were about redemption, not rebuke. The fellowship was a place where tears were honored, and testimonies encouraged.

Finding a permanent home for the fellowship wasn't easy. Early spaces came with more obstacles than open arms. One landlord even warned them, "You won't be happy here." And she was right. The heat blasted in summer; the A/C froze in winter. Still, Rev. Joe and First Lady Laverne remained faithful. They prayed. They persisted. And they preached when many others warned, "Don't bring convicts into your church."

But God makes a way out of no way.

They held Sunday services at the Holiday Inn, just a few miles from their home. The staff eventually came to know the members by name. The front desk would unlock the ballroom doors and smile, knowing there would be peace and praise within. After each service, volunteers stacked chairs, swept the floors, and welcomed newcomers with hugs. Children danced in the choir. Elders lifted holy hands. It wasn't the Ritz. But it was sacred.

Eventually, they purchased the little white church on the hill— 701 West Johnson Street. Small in square footage, vast in spirit. Bought and paid for—no mortgage.

Out of this Fellowship came something even bigger:

The Academy of Life (AOL)—an outreach ministry for those forgotten by systems and policies. AOL provided workshops in drug prevention, domestic violence, nutrition, job training, and reentry support. All volunteer-run. No salaries. Just heart. Former inmates came back, not just to say thanks—but to teach.

Rev. Joe even brokered a deal with Marriott Hotels: graduates of the job training program would get hiring preference. One woman, once homeless and battling addiction, completed the program and is now a manager at a downtown Marriott. Stories like hers fill the walls of Mount Airy United Fellowship like living stained glass windows.

Joe's sermons were never long-winded interpretations of scripture chapter and verse, but they were unforgettable.

"You want directions to get to Heaven? Make a Right and Go Straight."

"You can't make sense out of nonsense. But God can."

"Don't worry about who's in the White House. Worry about who's in Your House."

His words always landed with rhythm, almost like a refrain in a gospel song. He can stand flat-footed and deliver one-liners with the perfect pitch and timing just as any veteran of the stage would. They stirred laughter, reflection, and repentance. His sermons ended with a benediction and a to-do list—what God could do, yes, but also what you were now accountable for. He, would say, "I'm Just Doing what the Lord Say Do".

Even now, in his silver years, Joe hasn't slowed. He rises early, still accepts calls and request from members and long-time friends for prayer and comfort. He runs a conference call ministry born during the COVID shutdown.

Three times a week, the faithful dial in—former inmates, old friends, new believers. Each call opens with scripture, includes a song from Mama Laverne, and ends with Rev. Joe's signature "Word on the Street." And "Health Advisory," The Sunday call has become a lifeline for many, a digital altar call.

"Ask God for Protection and Direction," he reminds them.

# *What They Value & Are Proud Of*

Rev. Joe treasures his daughter, Cydney, and carries the memory of baby Joey like a hymn in his heart. He is the last living sibling of six. No regrets—only stories, miles, and souls touched. He often speaks about his siblings with great tenderness. Each one had a chapter in his story.

He never took a salary. Never sold chicken dinners to fund the church. "God always provided," he says. His work with the Dixie Hummingbirds—first as promoter, then as a full member—remains a badge of honor. He attended every homegoing of his beloved *Birds* as they each flew home to Glory. He still remembers every stage, every set list, and every face in the crowd. He recalled the irony of his relationship with James B. Davis and his son. "Interesting that I chose music and stayed with the Birds and my father taught Mr. Davis's son plumbing and that's where he built his career". It's odd how life turns out", he said.

Miss Laverne, the heartbeat of the fellowship, is the last of the Jones children from that Pennsylvania coal town. Her voice—rich and soul-stirring—needs no accompaniment. As she thinks of her sisters and brother, a tear can arrive almost on queue as she recounts stories of them and her parents.

A great baker, Laverne once baked a guitar-shaped cake for Howard Carroll, of the Birds and even made one for the Philadelphia Phillies' mascot, the Phanatic. Her gifts are many. Her humility is even greater. She has hosted bridal showers, baby dedications, and bereavement meals—all in the church basement. Her hands have prepared thousands of plates. Her prayers have lifted just as many souls.

Their love story—one of hills and valleys, grief and grace—is still being written. They often laugh at the way they met and the many obstacles they overcame. It's a story marked by faith, forgiveness, and fierce commitment.

"Flying with the Birds" has always meant more than music. It's a testimony of faith taking flight.

So, what's next?

No one knows for sure. There are whispers of podcasts. More outreach. A digital revival of sorts. There is talk of a mentorship circle. A traveling fellowship. Perhaps even a documentary. The story, like the gospel, continues to unfold.

But if you ask Rev. Joe, he'll simply smile and say:

*"When you can't, God can.*
*And when you won't, God will."*

Peace and Blessings,
Dr. Lynn Peterson

*Mount Airy United Fellowship 701 West Johnson St. Philadelphia, PA*

*Renewing Their Vows- 50th Anniversary*

*In the Chapel- Rev Joe, Mr. Barker, Hassan Camara*

*Commemorative Street Marker North Philadelphia*

# Honors & Accolades

Reverend Joe Williams, the remaining member of the *Dixie Hummingbirds*

- **Chaplin of AFRICAN AMERICAN Museum of Philadelphia, PA.**
- Chaplin of the **Charles L. Blockson Afro-American Collection Special Collections—African American Studies at Temple University**
- **Chaplin of The Clef Club the Philadelphia Clef Club of Jazz and Performing Arts** (PCC), founded in 1966, was one of the most significant events in the history of Musicians' Protective Union Local 274, American Federation of Musicians (AFM). Prof. Lovette Hines
- **Chaplin of the Paul Robeson House & Museum-Philadelphia,** PA. An American bass-baritone concert artist, actor, professional football player, and activist who became famous both for his cultural accomplishments and for his political stances. In his final years, he lived in Philadelphia. The Museum houses artifacts of his life. The West Philadelphia Cultural Alliance presents the exhibit.

- **National Endowment for the Arts Heritage** recognized the Dixie Hummingbirds' contribution to gospel music in 2000. Rev Joe Williams accepts the Award for the group.
- Living LEGENDS AWARD 2009
- Rev Joe presided at the placement of The Dixie Hummingbirds' artifacts at the **National Museum of African American History and Culture in Washington, D.C.**
- Rev Joe was the key member who initiated the **Historical Marker for the Dixie Hummingbirds**, placed at the home of Founder James B. Davis, 2435 College-Philadelphia, PA, June 2017.
- **The Times Herald**-Reverend Joe Williams celebrates his 80th Birthday at the African American Museum of Philadelphia -2017
- *PHILADELPHIA (CBS)* 2018-T**he Pew Center for the Arts & Heritage,** along with Rev Joe, told the story of how gospel music influenced the sound of rock as well as how the Grammy award-winning group Dixie Hummingbirds played a role in that evolution.
- **6abc Celebrates Black Music Month June 2023** during a rehearsal at Mt. Airy United Fellowship with Rev Joe & his wife Laverne Williams with *Philly Remembers*, a nonprofit

group of gospel singers, musicians, and composers from across Delaware Valley.

- Certificate of Appreciation: **Living Legend Awards 2009,** Personal contributions to Gospel Music Preservation.

- **Philadelphia Music Walk of Fame (c. 2017)**
  As one of the few living representatives of the group, Rev. Williams attended the Dixie Hummingbirds' induction ceremony, underscoring both his and the group's enduring connection to Philadelphia's musical history en.wikipedia.org+10youtube.com+10journalofgospelmusic. com+10.

- **Certificate of Appreciation (June 20, 2009)**
  On WLUW's "Gospel Memories" radio show, Rev. Williams honored gospel historian/historian Bob Marovich with a certificate recognizing his exceptional work in preserving and showcasing vintage gospel music journalofgospelmusic.com+1journalofgospelmusic.com+1.

- **"Living Legend Music Awards" Host (June 27, 2009)**
  Shortly after the radio show, Rev. Williams announced and hosted the inaugural Living Legend Music Awards in Philadelphia, aimed at honoring gospel music pioneers, journalofgospelmusic.com+1youtube.com+1.

- **Featured in Journal of Gospel Music Interview (May 4, 2017)**
  Artistically recognized in an extensive "Conversations with the Gospel Legends" interview. The feature highlighted his long career in both the Sons of the Birds and the Dixie Hummingbirds
  youtube.com+9journalofgospelmusic.com+9journalofgospelmusic.com+9.

- **Buffalo Soldiers Museum**- Galveston, TX. -Speaker at their Annual -20years as an Honorary Member.

- Honorary Member of the Triple Nickel-The "Triple Nickel" refers to the 555th Parachute Infantry Battalion, an all-Black unit in World War II. They were the first African American paratroopers in the U.S. Army, breaking racial barriers. Their legacy contributed to the eventual desegregation of the U.S. military.

- Member of the Philadelphia Ministers Alliance.

- **National Museum of African American Music**-NMAAM, **Nashville, TN,** is the only museum dedicated to preserving and celebrating the many music genres created, influenced, and inspired by African Americans. Displayed in the Museum, the suit worn by Rev Joe Williams of the Dixie Hummingbirds.

- Interim Minister for Enon Baptist Church for two years. Queen Lane location.

- Rev Joe was the Designated Recipient of the Commemorative Award for the late Sister Rosetta Tharpe on the *Philadelphia Walk of Fame 2017.*

- **The Philadelphia Music Alliance inducted the Dixie Hummingbirds into the Walk of Fame in 1988.**

*PHILADELPHIA (CBS) -Feb 27, 2018-* The Pew Center for the Arts & Heritage is helping tell the story of how gospel music helped influence the sound of rock as well as how the Grammy award-winning group Dixie Hummingbirds played a role in that evolution.

Rev. Joseph Williams, now the last living member of The Dixie Hummingbirds, discussed the Philadelphia premiere of "How They Got Over."

Williams detailed his time as a Dixie Hummingbird and how black gospel music shaped rock music and simultaneously helped heal a nation during the tumultuous civil rights era.

"Gospel music was the fuel that kept the buses running," he said. "Gave hope to hopeless people."

# Rev. Joe Quotes

1. *"Truth Is the Foundation That Facts Are Based Upon"*

2. *"You Have to Know What Kind of Weather You're Flying In"*

3. *"There Is a Difference Between Need & Greed"*

4. *"Take a Minute to Include GOD in It!"*

5. *"Go to Hell Your Way or Go to Heaven GOD's Way"*

6. *"Prayer Can Go Where You Are Trying to Go"*

7. *"Never Forget That a Half Truth Is a Whole lie"*

8. *"Remember to Give Yourself Enough Time to Be on Time!"*

9. *"History Does Not Raise Questions, It Answers Questions"*

10. *"Don't Expect Lost People to help you Find Yourself"*

11. *"We Are in the Fight of Our Lives, and GOD Is the Referee"*

12. *"You Can't Make Sense Out of Nonsense!"*

13. *"There is No Right Way to Do Wrong and No Wrong Way to Do Right!"*

14. *"Don't Worry About Who's in the White House, Worry About Who's in Your House"*

**15.** *"Do We ever Wonder if GOD Has Moved?"*

**16.** *"A Story About a Little Boy Sitting on the Steps of the Church Crying. Jesus Christ Saw the Boy and Asked Him, 'Why Are You Crying?' The Little Boy Said, 'They Won't Let Me in That Church.' Jesus Said, 'Don't Worry, They Won't Let Me in Either!'"*

**17.** *"It Didn't Cost You a Dime to Turn the Sun on This Morning"*

**18.** *"Stop Using BIG Words with Little Meanings"*

**19.** *"The Devil Doesn't Own Pajamas, He Never Sleeps"*

**20.** *"It's Not How High You Can Jump When You Shout. It's How Straight You Walk When You Come Down"*

**21.** *"We Are Gospel Hobos Even Though Our Father Is Rich with Houses & Land"*

**22.** *"When J.P. Getty Died, Someone Asked, 'How Much Did He Leave?' Someone replied, 'All of It!'"*

**23.** *"Try Walking with GOD Without Asking for Anything!"*

**24.** *"Orders Are Handed Down, Not Up"*

25. *"Try to Make a Difference"*

26. *"GOD Can Turn on the Sun. Ask HIM, 'What Will You Have Me Do Today?'"*

27. *"Just Because You Moved to the Suburbs Doesn't Mean the Devil Didn't Move with You"*

28. *"Directions to Heaven: Make a Right & Go Straight!"*

29. *"Whenever You Pray, Get Out of the Way and Let GOD Do It HIS Way"*

30. *"What Goes in the Wash Will Come Out in the Rinse"*

31. *"Only What We Do for Christ Will Last!"*

32. *"You Are Black Until Further Notice"*

33. *"GOD Is Not hard of Hearing"*

34. *"Plant the Trees Now So We Will Have Shade Later"*

35. *"Don't Serve People, Serve GOD"*

36. *"A Lie Can Outrun You & Wait"*

37. *"What Is Coming Is Better Than What Has Been"*

38. *"A Lie Will Go Around the World Twice Before the Truth Gets Out of Bed"*

**39.** *"Don't Let the Devil Ride with You, Eventually He Will Want to Drive"*

**40.** *"We're in the 9th Inning, Lord Help us!"*

**41.** *"Thank YOU, Will Make Room for More"*

**42.** *"I Want You to Be as Happy as a Termite in a Lumber Yard"*

**43.** *"Don't Put a Question Mark Where GOD Put a Period"*

**44.** *"Busy? You're About as Busy as a One Arm Paper Hanger"*

**45.** *"When the Devil Knocks on the Door, Let GOD Answer It"*

**46.** *"We Need Education, Not Indoctrination"*

**47.** *"And Remember, When You Can't, GOD Can & When You Won't, GOD Will"*

www.ingramcontent.com/pod-product-compliance
Lightning Source LLC
Chambersburg PA
CBHW051549120626
46551CB00013B/1440